·*Cooking for Today*·

MICROWAVE MEALS

Cooking for Today

MICROWAVE MEALS

WENDY LEE

||| •PARRAGON• |||

First published in Great Britain in 1996 by
Parragon Book Service Ltd
Unit 13–17
Avonbridge Trading Estate
Atlantic Road
Avonmouth
Bristol BS11 9QD

ISBN 0-7525-1806-2

Produced by Haldane Mason

Printed in Italy

Acknowledgements:
Art Direction: Ron Samuels
Editor: Michael Williams
Series Design: Pedro & Frances Prá-Lopez/Kingfisher Design, London
Page Design: Somewhere Creative
Photography: Joff Lee
Styling: Maria Kelly
Home Economist: Wendy Lee

Photographs on pages 6, 20, 34, 48 and 62 are reproduced by permission of
ZEFA Picture Library (UK) Ltd

Note:
Cup measurements in this book are for American cups. Tablespoons are assumed to be 15 ml.
Unless otherwise stated, milk is assumed to be full-fat, eggs are standard size 3, butter is unsalted (sweet), and pepper is freshly ground black pepper.

Contents

CHAPTER ONE

Soups

❋

Home-made soups are so easy to make and these recipes will give you guaranteed success. Microwave cooking will give your soups the maximum taste and colour the ingredients can produce.

More often than not soups form the first course of a meal, but when served with bread they can provide a very warming, satisfying and convenient lunch or supper. On a cold winter's night there is nothing more welcoming than a steaming bowl of soup.

Most soups freeze well, especially the puréed variety, which is a bonus when entertaining. You can prepare the soup weeks ahead, leaving plenty of time to concentrate on the other courses. It is always a good idea to keep a container of soup in your freezer. If guests arrive unexpectedly or you have not had time to buy anything for supper, it can be defrosted and reheated in your microwave oven in a matter of minutes.

As there is less evaporation of liquid than the more conventional methods, microwave soup recipes generally have less liquid added. Always make soups in a large casserole or bowl to prevent the liquid from boiling over. Soups should be seasoned at the end of cooking when the flavours are most concentrated.

Opposite: *Fresh vegetables make perfect soups and keep their colour and texture superbly.*

STEP 2

STEP 3

STEP 4

STEP 5

PARSNIP & STILTON (BLUE CHEESE) SOUP

Creamy parsnip soup with a subtle Stilton (blue cheese) flavour and a hint of sage, served topped with crispy croûtons.

SERVES 4
PREPARATION: 20 MINS,
  COOKING: 25 MINS 45 SECS

500 g/1 lb parsnips, diced
1 potato, diced
1 onion, chopped
30 g/1 oz/2 tbsp butter
450 ml/³/₄ pint/2 cups hot vegetable stock
450 ml/³/₄ pint/2 cups milk
1 dried bay leaf
175 g/6 oz Stilton (blue cheese)
4 tbsp crème fraîche or soured cream
2 tbsp chopped fresh sage
salt and pepper

CROUTONS:
25 g/1 oz/2 tbsp butter
paprika
2 slices bread, crusts removed

1 Place the parsnips, potato, onion and butter in a large bowl. Cover and cook on HIGH power for 10 minutes, stirring halfway through.

2 Pour on the stock and milk, and add the bay leaf. Cover and cook on HIGH power for 10 minutes, stirring after 5 minutes.

3 Crumble the cheese into the soup and stir until melted. Remove the bay leaf and allow the soup to stand, covered, for 5 minutes.

4 To make the croûtons, place the butter in a small bowl. Cook on HIGH power for 45 seconds until melted. Add a pinch of paprika. Cut each slice of bread into 25 squares. Toss the bread in the melted butter, then spread out on a flat plate. Cook on HIGH power for 2 minutes, stirring several times, until the croûtons are firm. Allow the croûtons to stand, uncovered, for 5 minutes before serving.

5 Strain the vegetables and reserve the liquid. Purée the vegetables with a little of the reserved liquid in a food processor or blender, until they are smooth and creamy. Alternatively, press through a sieve (strainer). Transfer the purée to a clean bowl, add the reserved liquid and mix well. Season to taste.

6 Stir the crème fraîche or soured cream into the soup. Reheat on HIGH power for 3–4 minutes. Stir in the sage. Serve in warmed bowls sprinkled with croûtons.

STEP 1

STEP 2

STEP 3

STEP 4

BACON, BEAN & GARLIC SOUP

A mouth-wateringly healthy vegetable, bean and bacon soup with a garlic flavour. Serve with chunks of granary or wholemeal (whole wheat) bread to make a filling appetizer or a midweek meal.

SERVES 4
PREPARATION: 18 MINS,
COOKING: 17 MINS

250 g/8 oz smoked back bacon slices
1 carrot, sliced thinly
1 celery stick, sliced thinly
1 onion, chopped
1 tbsp oil
3 garlic cloves, sliced
700 ml/1¼ pints/3 cups hot vegetable stock
200 g/7 oz can chopped tomatoes
1 tbsp chopped fresh thyme
about 425 g/14 oz can cannellini beans,
*   drained*
1 tbsp tomato purée (paste)
salt and pepper
grated Cheddar cheese to garnish

1 Chop 2 slices of the bacon and place in a bowl. Cook on HIGH power for 3–4 minutes until the fat runs and the bacon is well cooked. Stir the bacon halfway through cooking to separate the pieces. Transfer to a plate lined with kitchen towels and leave to cool. When cool, the bacon pieces should be crisp and dry.

2 Place the carrot, celery, onion and oil in a large bowl. Cover and cook on HIGH power for 4 minutes.

3 Chop the remaining bacon and add to the bowl with the garlic. Cover and cook on HIGH power for 2 minutes.

4 Add the stock, the contents of the can of tomatoes, the thyme, beans and tomato purée (paste). Cover and cook on HIGH power for 8 minutes, stirring halfway through.

5 Season to taste. Ladle the soup into warmed bowls and sprinkle with the crisp bacon and grated Cheddar cheese.

FREEZING

This soup does not freeze well.

TIP

For a more substantial soup you could add 60 g/2 oz cup small pasta shapes or short lengths of spaghetti when you add the stock and tomatoes. You will also need to add an extra 150 ml/¼ pint/⅔ cup vegetable stock.

STEP 1

STEP 2

STEP 4

STEP 5

LENTIL & CORIANDER (CILANTRO) SOUP

Tasty red lentil soup flavoured with chopped coriander (cilantro). The yogurt adds a light piquancy to the soup when it is stirred in at the end.

SERVES 4
PREPARATION: 15 MINS,
   COOKING: 22 MINS

30 g/1 oz/2 tbsp butter
1 onion, chopped finely
1 celery stick, chopped finely
1 large carrot, grated
1 dried bay leaf
250 g/8 oz/1 cup red lentils
1.25 litres/2 pints/5 cups hot vegetable or
   chicken stock
2 tbsp chopped fresh coriander (cilantro)
4 tbsp natural yogurt
salt and pepper
fresh coriander (cilantro) sprigs to garnish

1 Place the butter, onion and celery in a large bowl. Cover and cook on HIGH power for 3 minutes.

2 Add the carrot, bay leaf and lentils. Pour over the stock. Cover and cook on HIGH power for 15 minutes, stirring halfway through.

3 Remove from the microwave oven and leave to stand, covered, for 5 minutes.

4 Remove the bay leaf, then blend in batches in a food processor, until smooth. Alternatively, press the soup through a sieve (strainer).

5 Pour into a clean bowl. Season to taste and stir in the coriander (cilantro). Cover and cook on HIGH power for 4–5 minutes until piping hot.

6 Serve in warmed bowls. Stir 1 tablespoon of yogurt into each serving and garnish with sprigs of fresh coriander (cilantro).

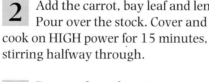

TIP

For an extra creamy soup try adding crème fraîche or soured cream instead of yogurt.

ORIENTAL FISH SOUP

This is a deliciously different fish soup made with haddock and strips of vegetable, and flavoured with soy sauce. Top with omelette shreds for a taste full of Eastern promise.

STEP 1

SERVES 4
PREPARATION: 15 MINS,
   COOKING 10 MINS

1 egg
1 tsp sesame seeds, toasted
1 celery stick, chopped
1 carrot, cut into julienne strips
4 spring onions (scallions), sliced on the
   diagonal
1 tbsp oil
60 g/ 2 oz/ 1¹/₂ cups fresh spinach
900 ml/ 1¹/₂ pints/ 3¹/₂ cups hot vegetable
   stock
4 tsp light soy sauce
250 g/ 8 oz haddock, skinned and cut into
   small chunks
salt and pepper

1 Beat the egg with the sesame seeds and seasoning. Lightly oil a plate and pour on the egg mixture. Cook on HIGH power for about 1¹/₂ minutes until just setting in the centre. Leave to stand for a few minutes before removing from the plate. Roll up the egg and shred thinly. Set aside.

2 Place the celery, carrot and spring onions (scallions) in a large bowl with the oil. Mix well. Cover and cook on HIGH power for 3 minutes.

3 Wash the spinach thoroughly. Discard any long stalks and drain well. Shred finely.

4 Add the hot stock, soy sauce, haddock and spinach to the vegetable mixture. Cover and cook on HIGH power for 5 minutes.

5 Stir the soup and season to taste. Serve in warmed bowls with the shredded egg scattered over.

STEP 1

FREEZING

This soup does not freeze well.

VARIATION

Instead of topping the soup with omelette shreds, you could pour the beaten egg, without the sesame seeds, into the hot stock at the end of the cooking time. The egg will set in pretty strands to give a flowery look.

STEP 2

STEP 4

BEETROOT & POTATO SOUP

A deep red soup of puréed beetroots and potatoes, this makes a stunning first course. Adding a swirl of soured cream and a few sprigs of dill gives a very pretty effect.

STEP 2

STEP 3

STEP 4

STEP 6

SERVES 4–6
PREPARATION: 20 MINS,
    COOKING 27 MINS

1 onion, chopped
350 g/12 oz potatoes, diced
1 small cooking apple, peeled, cored and
    grated
3 tbsp water
1 tsp cumin seeds
500 g/1 lb cooked beetroot, peeled and diced
1 dried bay leaf
pinch of dried thyme
1 tsp lemon juice
600 ml/1 pint/2½ cups hot vegetable stock
4 tbsp soured cream
salt and pepper
few sprigs of fresh dill to garnish

1 Place the onion, potatoes, apple and water in a large bowl. Cover and cook on HIGH power for 10 minutes.

2 Stir in the cumin seeds and cook on HIGH power for 1 minute.

3 Stir in the beetroot, bay leaf, thyme, lemon juice and stock. Cover and cook on HIGH power for 12 minutes, stirring halfway through.

4 Leave to stand, uncovered, for 5 minutes. Remove the bay leaf. Strain the vegetables and reserve the liquid. Purée the vegetables with a little of the reserved liquid in a food processor or blender, until they are smooth and creamy. Alternatively, either mash the soup or press it through a sieve (strainer).

5 Pour the vegetable purée into a clean bowl with the reserved liquid and mix well. Season to taste. Cover and cook on HIGH power for 4–5 minutes until piping hot.

6 Serve the soup in warmed bowls. Swirl 1 tablespoon of soured cream into each serving and garnish with a few sprigs of fresh dill.

TIP

To create a pretty swirl on your soup, use a teaspoon to make a spiral of soured cream in the centre of each serving. Drag a cocktail stick (toothpick) or skewer across the soured cream to give a feathered effect.

STEP 1

STEP 2

STEP 5

STEP 6

SPICED SWEDE (RUTABAGA) & CAULIFLOWER SOUP

A thick puréed soup flavoured with Indian spices and yogurt. Serve with hot naan bread.

SERVES 4
PREPARATION: 18 MINS,
  COOKING: 25 MINS

350 g/12 oz cauliflower, divided into small florets
350 g/12 oz swede (rutabaga), diced
1 onion, chopped
1 tbsp oil
3 tbsp water
1 garlic clove, crushed
2 tsp grated ginger root
1 tsp cumin seeds
1 tsp black mustard seeds
2 tsp ground coriander
2 tsp ground turmeric
900 ml/1½ pints/3½ cups hot vegetable stock
300 ml/½ pint/1¼ cups natural yogurt
salt and pepper
chopped fresh coriander (cilantro) to garnish

1 Place the cauliflower, swede (rutabaga), onion, oil and water in a large bowl. Cover and cook on HIGH power for 10 minutes, stirring halfway through.

2 Add the garlic, ginger and spices. Stir well, cover and cook on HIGH power for 2 minutes.

3 Pour in the stock, cover and cook on HIGH power for 10 minutes. Leave to stand, covered, for 5 minutes.

4 Strain the vegetables and reserve the liquid. Purée the vegetables with a little of the reserved liquid in a food processor or blender, until smooth and creamy. Alternatively, either mash the soup or press it through a sieve (strainer).

5 Pour the vegetable purée and remaining reserved liquid into a clean bowl and mix well. Season to taste.

6 Stir in the yogurt and cook on HIGH power for 3–4 minutes until hot but not boiling, otherwise the yogurt will curdle. Serve in warmed bowls garnished with chopped fresh coriander (cilantro).

HELPFUL HINTS

You can substitute 1 tablespoon of mild curry paste for all the spices if they are unavailable.

CHAPTER TWO

Starters & Light Meals

❦

For tempting starters or light meals, here is a selection of tasty dishes which are quick to prepare and tantalizing to the palate.

The flavour and texture of a starter should complement the main course. A light starter should precede a filling main course, otherwise your guests will be too full to appreciate the remainder of the meal. Whenever possible, prepare a recipe in advance, or at least to the stage where it can be quickly reheated in the microwave oven just before serving. Fondues can be fun, so for a lighthearted evening start the meal with a scrumptious cheese fondue.

Starters should be eye-catching; brightly coloured garnishes such as sprigs of herbs, or a few pretty lettuce leaves will add a delicate sophisticated touch.

A light meal, lunch or quick supper does not have to take a long time to prepare. Gone are the days of slaving over a hot stove. For those of us who lead busy lives a microwave oven is the perfect answer. So, rather than cooking the usual jacket potato or reheating a frozen pizza, treat yourself to one of these delicious recipes.

Opposite: *Fish dishes make ideal light meals and stay moist and full of flavour in the microwave oven.*

STEP 1

STEP 4

STEP 5

STEP 6

SPICED KIDNEYS

Lamb's kidneys and bacon cooked in a chilli-spiced sherry sauce. Serve with rice to give a full-flavoured light meal or first course.

SERVES 4
PREPARATION: 15 MINS,
   COOKING: 33 MINS

175 g/6 oz/scant cup long-grain rice
550 ml/18 fl oz/2¼ cups boiling water
8 lamb's kidneys, skinned, halved and cored
30 g/1 oz/2 tbsp butter
1 small onion, sliced
2 tbsp plain (all-purpose) flour
1 tsp chilli powder
2 slices back bacon, chopped
4 tbsp medium dry sherry
2 tbsp water
2 tbsp double (heavy) cream
salt and pepper
chopped fresh parsley to garnish

1 Place the rice in a large bowl. Pour over the boiling water. Add ½ teaspoon of salt. Cover and cook on HIGH power for 14 minutes, stirring from time to time until the rice is tender and the water has been absorbed. Leave to stand, covered, while cooking the kidneys.

2 Cut each kidney half into 3 and rinse in cold water. Drain well.

3 Place the butter and onion in a large bowl. Cover and cook on HIGH power for 2 minutes.

4 Mix the flour, chilli powder and seasoning in a bowl. Add the kidneys and toss well to coat. Add the kidneys and bacon to the onion. Cover and cook on HIGH power for 4 minutes.

5 Mix the sherry with the water. Stir into the kidney mixture, cover and cook on MEDIUM power for 15 minutes until the kidneys are tender.

6 Stir in the cream and adjust the seasoning. Garnish with parsley and serve with the rice.

TIP

Place the flour and seasonings in a large plastic bag, add the kidneys in batches and shake well to coat them evenly.

STEP 1

STEP 2

STEP 4

STEP 5

CAPELLINI & ROQUEFORT (BLUE CHEESE) POTS

A layered pasta and Parma (prosciutto) ham delight, beautifully complemented by a fresh tomato and basil sauce.

SERVES 4
PREPARATION: 30 MINS,
COOKING: 18 MINS

1 small onion, chopped
1 garlic clove, chopped
1 tbsp olive oil
4 tomatoes, skinned (see page 26) and chopped
1 tbsp tomato purée (paste)
4 fresh basil leaves, chopped
30 g/1 oz/2 tbsp butter
15 g/$^1\!/_2$ oz/2 tbsp dried brown breadcrumbs
15 g/$^1\!/_2$ oz/2 tbsp chopped hazelnuts, lightly toasted
90 g/3 oz dried cappellini pasta
15 g/$^1\!/_2$ oz/2 tbsp plain (all-purpose) flour
150 ml/$^1\!/_4$ pint/$^2\!/_3$ cup milk
30 g/1 oz Roquefort (blue) cheese
about 75 g/2$^1\!/_2$ oz Parma ham, chopped
4 pitted black olives, chopped
salt and pepper
sprigs of fresh basil to garnish

1 Place the onion, garlic and oil in a bowl. Cover and cook on HIGH power for 3 minutes. Add the tomatoes and tomato purée (paste) and cook on HIGH power for 4 minutes, stirring halfway through. Add the basil and seasoning. Leave to stand, covered, while making the capellini pots.

2 Place half the butter in a small bowl and cook on HIGH power for 30 seconds until melted. Brush inside 4 ramekin dishes with the melted butter. Mix the breadcrumbs and hazelnuts and coat the insides of the ramekins. Set aside.

3 Break the pasta into 3 short lengths and place in a large bowl. Pour over enough boiling water to cover the pasta by 2.5 cm/1 inch, and salt lightly. Cover and cook on HIGH power for 4 minutes, stirring halfway through. Leave to stand, covered, for 1 minute, then drain.

4 Place the remaining butter, the flour and milk in a small bowl. Cook on HIGH power for 2–2$^1\!/_2$ minutes until thickened, stirring well every 30 seconds. Crumble the cheese into sauce and stir until melted. Season to taste.

5 Add the pasta to sauce and mix well. Divide half the pasta mixture between the ramekins and top with the ham and olives. Spoon the remaining pasta mixture on top. Cook on MEDIUM power for 6 minutes. Leave to stand, uncovered, for 2 minutes before carefully turning out on to serving plates with some tomato sauce. Garnish with basil.

MUSSELS WITH TOMATO SAUCE

Mediterranean-style baked mussels topped with a fresh tomato sauce and breadcrumbs. Serve with chunks of bread to soak up any juices.

STEP 3

STEP 5

STEP 6

STEP 6

SERVES 2–4
PREPARATION: 25 MINS,
COOKING: 9 MINS

½ small onion, chopped
1 garlic clove, crushed
1 tbsp olive oil
3 tomatoes
1 tbsp chopped fresh parsley
900 g / 2 lb live mussels
1 tbsp freshly grated Parmesan cheese
1 tbsp fresh white breadcrumbs
salt and pepper
chopped fresh parsley to garnish

1 Place the onion, garlic and oil in a bowl. Cover and cook on HIGH power for 3 minutes.

2 Cut a cross in the base of each tomato and place them in a small bowl. Pour on boiling water and leave for about 45 seconds. Drain and then plunge into cold water. The skins will slide off easily. Chop the tomatoes, removing any hard cores.

3 Add the tomatoes to the onion mixture, cover and cook on HIGH power for 3 minutes. Stir in the parsley and season to taste.

4 Scrub the mussels well in several changes of cold water. Remove the beards and discard any open mussels and those which do not close when tapped smartly with the back of a knife.

5 Place the mussels in a large bowl. Add enough boiling water to cover them. Cover and cook on HIGH power for 2 minutes, stirring halfway through, until the mussels open. Drain well and remove the empty half of each shell. Arrange the mussels in 1 layer on a plate.

6 Spoon the tomato sauce over each mussel. Mix the Parmesan cheese with the breadcrumbs and sprinkle on top. Cook, uncovered, on HIGH power for 2 minutes. Garnish with parsley and serve.

TIP

Dry out the breadcrumbs in the microwave for an extra crunchy topping. Spread them on a plate and cook on HIGH power for 2 minutes, stirring once. Leave to stand uncovered.

AVOCADO MARGHERITA

Red tomatoes, green basil and white Mozzarella cheese make up the colours of the Italian flag, which is why this baked avocado recipe takes its name from the classic pizza.

STEP 1

SERVES 4
PREPARATION: 10 MINS,
    COOKING: 7 MINS

1 small red onion, sliced
1 garlic clove, crushed
1 tbsp olive oil
2 small tomatoes
2 avocados, halved and pitted
4 fresh basil leaves, torn into shreds
60 g/2 oz Mozzarella cheese, sliced thinly
salt and pepper

TO GARNISH:
mixed salad
fresh basil leaves

1 Place the onion, garlic and the olive oil in a bowl. Cover and cook on HIGH power for 2 minutes.

2 Meanwhile skin the tomatoes by cutting a cross in the base of the tomatoes and placing them in a small bowl. Pour on boiling water and leave for about 45 seconds. Drain and then plunge into cold water. The skins will slide off without too much difficulty.

3 Arrange the avocado halves on a plate with the narrow ends pointed

towards the centre. Spoon the onions into the hollow of each half.

4 Cut and slice the tomatoes in half. Divide the tomatoes, basil and thin slices of Mozzarella between the avocado halves. Season with salt and pepper.

5 Cook on MEDIUM power for 5 minutes until avocados are heated through and the cheese has melted. Serve garnished with basil leaves.

STEP 2

STEP 3

COMBINATION MICROWAVE OVENS WITH GRILL (BROILER)

Arrange the avocados on the low rack of the grill (broiler), or on the glass turntable. Cook on combination grill (broiler) 1 and LOW power for 8 minutes until browned and bubbling.

STEP 4

STEP 2

STEP 3

STEP 4

STEP 5

THREE-CHEESE FONDUE

A hot cheese dip made from three different cheeses. It is perfect with chunks of French bread and crisp raw vegetables.

SERVES 4
PREPARATION: 10 MINS,
  COOKING: 9 MINS

1 garlic clove
300 ml/¹/₂ pint/1¹/₄ cups dry white wine
250 g/8 oz/2 cups mild Cheddar cheese,
  grated
125 g/4 oz/1 cup Gruyère (Swiss) cheese,
  grated
125 g/4 oz/1 cup Mozzarella cheese, grated
2 tbsp cornflour (cornstarch)
pepper

TO SERVE:
French bread
vegetables, such as courgettes (zucchini),
  mushrooms, baby sweetcorn, and
  cauliflower

1 Bruise the garlic by placing the flat side of a knife on top and pressing down with the heel of your hand.

2 Rub the garlic around the inside of a large bowl. Discard the garlic. Pour the wine into the bowl and heat, uncovered, on HIGH power for 3–4 minutes until hot but not boiling.

3 Gradually add the Cheddar and Gruyère (Swiss) cheeses, stirring

well after each addition, then add the Mozzarella cheese. Stir until melted.

4 Mix the cornflour (cornstarch) with a little water and stir into the cheese mixture. Season with pepper.

5 Cover and cook on MEDIUM power for 6 minutes, stirring twice during cooking, until the sauce is smooth.

6 To serve, keep warm over a spirit lamp or reheat as necessary in the microwave oven. Dip in cubes of French bread and slices or florets of vegetables.

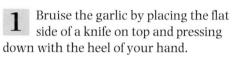

TIP

Make sure you add the cheese to the wine gradually, mixing well in between each addition, otherwise the mixture might curdle.

STEP 1

STEP 3

STEP 4

STEP 5

MARINATED CHICKEN KEBABS

Pieces of chicken marinated in yogurt, chutney and spices make meltingly tender kebabs.

SERVES 4
PREPARATION: 15 MINS,
 MARINATING: 1 HR,
 COOKING: 6 MINS

1 tbsp peach chutney
3 tbsp natural yogurt
$\frac{1}{2}$ tsp ground cumin
pinch of mixed (apple pie) spice
squeeze of lemon juice
3 chicken breast fillets, cut into even pieces
$\frac{1}{2}$ red (bell) pepper, cut into 16 even chunks
1 courgette (zucchini), cut into 16 slices
8 button mushrooms
salt and pepper

CHIVE & MINT DRESSING
150 ml/$\frac{1}{4}$ pint/$\frac{2}{3}$ cup natural yogurt
2 tbsp mayonnaise
2 tbsp milk
1 tbsp chopped fresh chives
1 tbsp chopped fresh mint

TO GARNISH:
sprigs of fresh mint
fresh chives
mixed salad to serve

1 Mix the chutney, yogurt, spices and lemon juice together in a bowl. Season to taste.

2 Add the chicken to the bowl. Mix well and leave in a cool place to marinate for 1 hour.

3 Thread the red (bell) pepper, courgette (zucchini), chicken and mushrooms on to 8 long wooden skewers.

4 Arrange 4 skewers on a large plate or microwave rack. Cook on HIGH power for 6 minutes, turning over and rearranging halfway through. Repeat with the remaining 4 kebabs.

5 To make the chive and mint dressing, mix together all the ingredients and season to taste.

6 Spoon the dressing over the kebabs and garnish with mint and chives.

COMBINATION MICROWAVE OVENS WITH GRILL (BROILER)

Thread the chicken and vegetables on to metal skewers. Arrange 4 kebabs on the grill (broiler) accessory and brush lightly with oil. Grill (broil) on the highest setting for 15–18 minutes, turning several times. Repeat with the remaining 4 skewers.

CHAPTER THREE

Main Meals

❦

There are so many delightful main courses to be made in the microwave oven, from a variety of pasta dishes topped with creamy sauces, to spicy Mexican-style beef, chicken curries and bacon chops stuffed with lentils and apricots.

Fish cooks superbly in the microwave oven, staying moist and full of flavour. When cooking meat, choose good quality, lean, tender cuts. Remove as much fat as possible beforehand and remember that overcooking will give a tough, rubbery result.

As microwave ovens do not brown food, add as much colour as possible to any dish by using a wide variety of fresh fruit and vegetables. A recipe which is usually a golden brown when cooked by conventional methods can often be finished off by placing it under a hot grill for a few minutes to obtain the desired effect.

Cooking in a combination oven will give you the best of both worlds. The microwave oven reduces the overall cooking time while the oven or grill (broiler) give you the traditional browning and crispness.

Opposite: Fresh chillies give spicy main dishes an added fieriness, but remember to be careful to avoid touching your eyes when preparing them.

FRUITY STUFFED BACON CHOPS

A combination of green lentils, celery and apricots stuffed into 'pockets' cut in bacon chops, served with a light orange and apricot sauce, makes a speedy meal.

STEP 1

STEP 2

STEP 4

STEP 5

SERVES 4
PREPARATION: 20 MINS,
COOKING: 28 MINS

60 g/2 oz/¹/₄ cup green lentils, washed
1 celery stick, sliced
2 spring onions (scallions), chopped
4 thick cut tendersweet bacon chops
1 tbsp chopped fresh sage
4 apricot halves canned in natural juice,
    drained and chopped
1 tsp cornflour (cornstarch)
4 tbsp natural juice from can of apricots
2 tbsp fresh orange juice
1 tsp grated orange rind
1 tbsp crème fraîche or soured cream
salt and pepper

TO GARNISH:
orange slices
sprigs of fresh sage

1 Place the lentils and celery in a bowl. Pour on boiling water to cover them. Cover and cook on HIGH power for 18–20 minutes until tender, adding extra water if necessary. Add the spring onions (scallions) for the last minute of cooking. Leave to stand, covered, for 10 minutes.

2 Using a sharp knife, slit the meaty end of each chop nearly through to the fat side, to form a pocket.

3 Drain the lentils and mix with half of the sage and the apricots. Season to taste.

4 Spoon the lentil stuffing into the pockets in the bacon chops. Arrange 2 on a plate. Cover with a paper towel. Cook on HIGH power for 4 minutes until cooked through. Transfer to warmed plates, cover and keep warm while cooking the remaining stuffed chops.

5 Mix the cornflour (cornstarch) with a little water in a bowl, then stir in the juice from the apricots, and the orange juice and rind. Cover and cook on HIGH power for 2 minutes, stirring every 30 seconds. Stir in the crème fraîche or soured cream and remaining sage. Season to taste and reheat on HIGH power for 30 seconds.

6 Serve the bacon chops with the sauce spooned over. Garnish with orange slices and sprigs of fresh sage.

CHICKEN & COCONUT CURRY

Tender chunks of chicken in a creamy curry sauce, delicately flavoured with coconut.

STEP 2

STEP 2

STEP 4

STEP 5

SERVES 4
PREPARATION: 15 MINS,
  COOKING: 17 MINS

1 onion, sliced
2 tbsp oil
2 tsp garam masala
1 tsp ground turmeric
1 tsp ground cumin
1 dried bay leaf
1 garlic clove, crushed
1 fresh green chilli, deseeded and chopped
4 chicken breast fillets, cut into chunks
4 tomatoes, skinned (see page 26)
1/2 green (bell) pepper, cut into chunks
150 ml/1/4 pint/2/3 cup coconut milk
2 tsp cornflour (cornstarch)
1 tbsp chopped fresh coriander (cilantro)
salt

TO SERVE:
boiled rice
poppadoms
chutney

1 Place the onion and oil in a large bowl. Cover and cook on HIGH power for 2 minutes.

2 Add the garam masala, turmeric, cumin, bay leaf, garlic and chilli. Cover and cook on HIGH power for 1 minute. Stir in the chicken, cover and cook on HIGH power for 4 minutes, stirring halfway through.

3 Cut each tomato into 6 wedges, removing any hard cores.

4 Add the tomatoes, (bell) pepper and coconut milk to the chicken. Mix the cornflour (cornstarch) with a little water, then stir into the bowl. Season with salt, cover and cook on MEDIUM power for 10 minutes.

5 Stir in the coriander (cilantro). Adjust the seasoning and serve with rice, poppadoms and chutney.

COMBINATION

Cover and cook on combination convection 160°C/325°F and WARM power for 1 hour until the chicken is tender.

CHILLIES

Take care when using fresh chillies: handle them as little as possible and avoid touching your eyes or any cuts and bruises. When you have finished, wash your hands well.

MEXICAN BEEF

Strips of beef cooked with (bell) peppers and onion and carrot in a tomato and chilli sauce are served with brown rice, tortillas and salsa.

STEP 1

SERVES 4
PREPARATION: 20 MINS,
   COOKING: 32 MINS

250 g/8 oz/1 generous cup brown rice
700 ml/1¼ pints/3 cups boiling water
½ tsp salt
2 tbsp oil
1 onion, sliced into rings
1 carrot, cut into thin matchsticks
½ each red, green and yellow (bell) peppers,
   sliced
½–1 fresh green chilli, deseeded and chopped
1 garlic clove, crushed
500 g/1 lb rump steak, cut into strips
225 g/7 oz/scant 1 cup canned tomatoes
1 tbsp tomato purée (paste)
2 tsp cornflour (cornstarch)
sprigs of fresh coriander (cilantro) to
   garnish

SALSA:
2 tomatoes, skinned (see page 26) and
   chopped
2 spring onions (scallions), chopped
1 small fresh green chilli, deseeded and
   chopped
2 tbsp lime juice
1 tbsp chopped fresh coriander (cilantro)
8 flour tortillas
salt and pepper

1 Place the rice in a large bowl. Add the boiling water and salt. Cover and cook on HIGH power for 15 minutes. Leave to stand, covered, for 5 minutes before draining.

2 Place the oil, onion and carrot in a large bowl. Cover and cook on HIGH power for 2 minutes. Add the (bell) peppers, chilli, garlic and steak. Cover and cook on HIGH power for 4 minutes, stirring once.

3 Add the canned tomatoes, tomato purée (paste) and seasoning. Mix the cornflour (cornstarch) with a little water, then stir into the bowl. Cover and cook on MEDIUM power for 10 minutes.

4 To make the salsa, mix together the tomatoes, spring onions (scallions), chilli, lime juice and coriander (cilantro). Season to taste and leave to stand for 10 minutes.

5 Heat the tortillas on HIGH power for 40 seconds, covered or according to the packet instructions.

6 Garnish the beef with fresh coriander (cilantro) sprigs and serve with the tortillas, rice and salsa.

STEP 2

STEP 3

STEP 4

STEP 1

STEP 3

STEP 4

STEP 5

SALMON & MUSHROOM LASAGNE ROLLS

Sheets of green lasagne are rolled and filled with a mixture of fresh salmon and oyster mushrooms, topped with a bubbling white sauce, Parmesan cheese and breadcrumbs.

SERVES 4
PREPARATION: 30 MINS,
COOKING: 20 MINS

8 sheets green lasagne
1 onion, sliced
15 g/¹/₂ oz/ 1 tbsp butter
¹/₂ red (bell) pepper, chopped
1 courgette (zucchini), diced
1 tsp chopped ginger root
125 g/4 oz oyster mushrooms, preferably
* yellow, chopped coarsely*
250 g/8 oz fresh salmon fillet, skinned, and
* cut into chunks*
2 tbsp dry sherry
2 tsp cornflour (cornstarch)
20 g/³/₄ oz/ 3 tbsp plain (all-purpose) flour
20 g/³/₄ oz/ 1¹/₂ tbsp butter
300 ml/¹/₂ pint/ 1¹/₄ cups milk
30 g/ 1 oz/¹/₄ cup Cheddar cheese, grated
15 g/¹/₂ oz/¹/₄ cup fresh white breadcrumbs
salt and pepper
salad to serve

1 Place the lasagne sheets in a large shallow dish. Cover with plenty of boiling water. Cook on HIGH power for 5 minutes. Leave to stand, covered, for a few minutes before draining. Rinse in cold water and lay the sheets out on a clean work surface.

2 Put the onion and butter into a bowl. Cover and cook on HIGH power for 2 minutes. Add the (bell) pepper, courgette (zucchini) and ginger root. Cover and cook on HIGH power for 3 minutes.

3 Add the mushrooms and salmon to the bowl. Mix the sherry into the cornflour (cornstarch) then stir into the bowl. Cover and cook on HIGH power for 4 minutes until the fish flakes when tested with a fork. Season to taste.

4 Whisk the flour, butter and milk in a bowl. Cook on HIGH power for 3–4 minutes, whisking every minute, to give a sauce of coating consistency. Stir in half the cheese and season to taste.

5 Spoon the salmon filling in equal quantities along the shorter side of each lasagne sheet. Roll up to enclose the filling. Arrange in a lightly oiled large rectangular dish. Pour over the sauce and sprinkle over the remaining cheese and the breadcrumbs.

6 Cook on HIGH power for 3 minutes until heated through. If possible, lightly brown under a preheated grill (broiler) before serving. Serve with salad.

PASTA & LAMB LOAF

A delicious lamb and aubergine (eggplant) pasta loaf which could be made using any dried pasta shape. Serve hot or cold at picnics or for lunch.

STEP 2

STEP 4

STEP 5

STEP 5

SERVES 3–4
PREPARATION: 20 MINS,
  COOKING: 25 MINS

15 g/¹/₂ oz/1 tbsp butter
¹/₂ small aubergine (eggplant), diced
60 g/2 oz multi-coloured fusilli
2 tsp olive oil
250 g/8 oz/1 cup minced (ground) lamb
¹/₂ small onion, chopped
¹/₂ red (bell) pepper, chopped
1 garlic clove, crushed
1 tsp dried mixed herbs
2 eggs, beaten
2 tbsp single (light) cream
salt and pepper

TO SERVE:
salad
pasta sauce of your choice

1 Place the butter in a 500 g/1 lb loaf dish. Cook on HIGH power for 30 seconds until melted. Brush over the base and sides. Sprinkle the aubergine (eggplant) with salt, put in a colander and leave to drain over a sink for about 20 minutes. Rinse the aubergine (eggplant) well and pat dry with paper towels.

2 Place the pasta in a bowl, add a little salt and boiling water to cover by 2.5 cm/1 inch. Cover and cook on HIGH power for 8 minutes, stirring halfway through. Leave to stand, covered, for a few minutes.

3 Place the oil, lamb and onion in a bowl. Cover and cook on HIGH power for 2 minutes.

4 Break up any lumps of meat using a fork. Add the (bell) pepper, garlic, herbs and aubergine (eggplant). Cover and cook on HIGH power for 5 minutes, stirring.

5 Drain the pasta and add to the lamb with the eggs and cream. Season well. Turn into the loaf dish and pat down using the back of a spoon.

6 Cook on MEDIUM power for 10 minutes until firm to the touch. Leave to stand for 5 minutes before turning out. Serve in slices with a salad and a ready made pasta sauce.

STEP 1

STEP 2

STEP 3

STEP 5

PENNE WITH BUTTERNUT SQUASH & HAM

Squashes are becoming increasingly popular and readily available. The creamy, nutty flavour of butternut squash complements the 'al dente' texture of the pasta perfectly.

SERVES 4
PREPARATION: 15 MINS,
   COOKING: 24 MINS

2 tbsp olive oil
1 garlic clove, crushed
60 g/2 oz/1 cup fresh white breadcrumbs
500 g/1 lb peeled and deseeded butternut
   squash
8 tbsp water
500 g/1 lb fresh penne, or other pasta shape
15 g/¹/₂ oz/1 tbsp butter
1 onion, sliced
125 g/4 oz/¹/₂ cup ham, cut into strips
200 ml/7 fl oz/scant cup single (light)
   cream
60 g/2 oz/¹/₂ cup Cheddar cheese, grated
2 tbsp chopped fresh parsley
salt and pepper

1 Mix together the oil, garlic and breadcrumbs and spread out on a large plate. Cook on HIGH power for 4–5 minutes, stirring every minute, until crisp and beginning to brown. Set aside.

2 Dice the squash. Place in a large bowl with half the water. Cover and cook on HIGH power for 8–9 minutes, stirring occasionally. Leave to stand for 2 minutes.

3 Place the pasta in a large bowl, add a little salt and pour over boiling water to cover by 2.5 cm/1 inch. Cover and cook on HIGH power for 5 minutes, stirring once, until the pasta is just tender but still firm to the bite. Leave to stand, covered, for 1 minute before draining.

4 Place the butter and onion in a large bowl. Cover and cook on HIGH power for 3 minutes.

5 Coarsely mash the squash, using a fork. Add to the onion with the pasta, ham, cream, cheese, parsley and remaining water. Season generously and mix well. Cover and cook on HIGH power for 4 minutes until heated through.

6 Serve the pasta sprinkled with the crisp garlic crumbs.

TIP

If the squash weighs more than is needed for this recipe, blanch the excess for 3–4 minutes on HIGH power in a covered bowl with a little water. Drain, cool and place in a freezer bag. Store in the freezer for up to 3 months.

CHAPTER FOUR

Vegetarian Meals

❦

It has to be said that vegetables are the most successful of foods cooked in the microwave oven. The maximum colour and flavour are retained, as very little water is added when cooking. For this reason, and also because of the shortened cooking times, the vegetable colours do not fade and nutrients are not lost in an excess of boiling water. The natural moisture present in the vegetables creates a certain amount of steam, so only a few tablespoons of water need be added.

Keep vegetables covered during cooking to keep in the steam so the vegetables remain tender and do not dry out. Always remember to remove the cover away from you when allowing the steam to escape at the end of the cooking time.

Textures remain perfect, vegetables keep their shape and do not become soggy. Cut vegetables into similar-sized pieces or slices to ensure even cooking. Always choose the best quality vegetables and herbs to give maximum flavour.

Cooking pasta and rice in the microwave oven will not save you time but it will spare the washing up of messy pans. Rice grains have a light, fluffy texture and stay separate. Make accompanying pasta sauces while the pasta is still cooking.

Opposite: *Vegetables cooked in the microwave retain more of their flavour and goodness than with conventional methods of cooking.*

STEP 1

STEP 2

STEP 4

STEP 5

STUFFED GLOBE ARTICHOKES

Instead of serving artichokes with the usual mayonnaise or vinaigrette, fill the centres with a delicious pine kernel (nut), sun-dried tomato, olive and mushroom stuffing.

SERVES 4
PREPARATION: 25 MINS,
  COOKING: 31 MINS

4 globe artichokes
8 tbsp water
4 tbsp lemon juice
1 onion, chopped
1 garlic clove, crushed
2 tbsp olive oil
250 g/8 oz/2 cups button mushrooms,
  chopped
40 g/1½ oz pitted black olives, sliced
60 g/2 oz/¼ cup sun-dried tomatoes in oil,
  drained and chopped
1 tbsp chopped fresh basil
60 g/2 oz/1 cup fresh white breadcrumbs
30 g/1 oz/¼ cup pine kernels (nuts),
  toasted
oil from the jar of sun-dried tomatoes for
  drizzling
salt and pepper

1 Cut the stalks and lower leaves off the artichokes. Snip off the leaf tips using scissors. Place 2 artichokes in a large bowl with half the water and half the lemon juice. Cover and cook on HIGH power for 10 minutes, turning the artichokes over halfway through, until a leaf pulls away easily from the base. Leave to stand, covered, for 3 minutes before draining. Turn the artichokes upside down and leave to cool. Repeat with the remaining artichokes.

2 Place the onion, garlic and oil in a bowl. Cover and cook on HIGH power for 2 minutes, stirring once. Add the mushrooms, olives and sun-dried tomatoes. Cover and cook on HIGH power for 2 minutes.

3 Stir in the basil, breadcrumbs and pine kernels (nuts). Season to taste.

4 Turn the artichokes the right way up and carefully pull the leaves apart. Remove the purple-tipped central leaves. Using a teaspoon, scrape out the hairy choke and discard.

5 Divide the stuffing into 4 and spoon into the centre of each artichoke. Push the leaves back around the stuffing.

6 Arrange in a shallow dish and drizzle over a little oil from the jar of sun-dried tomatoes. Cook on HIGH power for 7–8 minutes to reheat, turning the artichokes around halfway through.

STEP 2

STEP 2

STEP 3

STEP 4

GREEN RISOTTO

A simple and quick rice dish cooked with green vegetables and herbs and served with shaved Parmesan cheese. Serve either as a first course for four people or a main course for two.

SERVES 2–4
PREPARATION: 12 MINS,
COOKING: 16 MINS

1 onion, chopped
2 tbsp olive oil
250 g/8 oz/generous 1 cup risotto rice
700 ml/1¼ pints/3 cups hot vegetable stock
350 g/12 oz mixed green vegetables, such as asparagus, thin green beans, mangetout (snow peas), courgettes (zucchini), broccoli florets, frozen peas
2 tbsp chopped fresh parsley
60 g/2 oz/¼ cup fresh Parmesan cheese, shaved thinly
salt and pepper

1 Place the onion and oil in a large bowl. Cover and cook on HIGH power for 2 minutes.

2 Add the rice and stir until thoroughly coated in the oil. Pour in about 75 ml/3 fl oz/⅓ cup of the hot stock. Cook, uncovered, for 2 minutes, until the liquid has been absorbed. Pour in another 75 ml/3 fl oz/⅓ cup of the stock and cook, uncovered, on HIGH power for 2 minutes. Repeat once more.

3 Chop or slice the vegetables into even-sized pieces. Stir into the rice

with the remaining stock. Cover and cook on HIGH power for 8 minutes, stirring occasionally, until most of the liquid has been absorbed and the rice is just tender.

4 Stir in the parsley and season generously. Leave to stand, covered, for almost 5 minutes. The rice should be tender and creamy.

5 Scatter the Parmesan cheese over before serving.

TIP

For extra texture, stir in a few toasted pine kernels (nuts) or coarsely chopped cashew nuts at the end of the cooking time.

TOFU (BEAN CURD) & VEGETABLES WITH BLACK BEAN SAUCE

Chunks of tofu (bean curd) are marinated in soy sauce and sherry, then stir-fried with egg noodles and colourful vegetables with black bean sauce and served with egg noodles.

STEP 1

SERVES 4
PREPARATION: 15 MINS,
    COOKING: 11 MINS

285 g/9½ oz smoked tofu (bean curd),
    cubed
2 tbsp soy sauce
1 tbsp dry sherry
1 tsp sesame oil
4 dried Chinese mushrooms
250 g/8 oz egg noodles
1 carrot, cut into thin sticks
1 celery stick, cut into thin sticks
125 g/4 oz (16–18) baby sweetcorn,
    halved lengthwise
2 tbsp oil
1 courgette (zucchini), sliced
4 spring onions (scallions), chopped
125 g/4 oz/1⅓ cups mangetout (snow
    peas), each cut into 3 pieces
2 tbsp black bean sauce
1 tsp cornflour (cornstarch)
salt and pepper
1 tbsp toasted sesame seeds to garnish

1 Marinate the tofu (bean curd) in the soy sauce, sherry and sesame oil for 30 minutes.

2 Place the mushrooms in a small bowl and pour over boiling water to cover. Leave to soak for 20 minutes.

3 Place the egg noodles in a large bowl. Pour over enough boiling water to cover by 2.5 cm/1 inch. Add ½ teaspoon salt, cover and cook on HIGH power for 4 minutes.

4 Place the carrot, celery, sweetcorn and oil in a large bowl. Cover and cook on HIGH power for 1 minute. Drain the mushrooms, reserving 1 tablespoon of the liquid. Squeeze out excess water from the mushrooms and discard the hard cores. Thinly slice the mushrooms.

5 Add to the bowl of vegetables with the courgette (zucchini), spring onions (scallions) and mangetout (snow peas). Mix well. Cover and cook on HIGH power for 4 minutes, stirring every minute.

6 Add the black bean sauce. Mix the cornflour (cornstarch) with reserved mushroom water and stir into the vegetables with the tofu (bean curd) and marinade. Cover and cook on HIGH power for 2–3 minutes until heated through and sauce has thickened slightly. Season to taste. Drain the noodles. Garnish the vegetables with sesame seeds and serve with the noodles.

STEP 4

STEP 5

STEP 6

STEP 1

STEP 2

STEP 4

STEP 6

BABY CAULIFLOWERS WITH POPPY SEED SAUCE

Whole baby cauliflowers coated with a red Leicester cheese and poppy seed sauce. Serve either as a tasty main course or as a side dish.

SERVES 4
PREARATION: 12 MINS,
    COOKING: 13 MINS

4 cloves
½ onion
½ carrot
1 bouquet garni
250 ml/ 8 fl oz/ 1 cup milk
4 baby cauliflowers
3 tbsp water
15 g/ ½ oz/ 1 tbsp butter
15 g/ ½ oz/ 1 tbsp plain (all-purpose) flour
60 g/ 2 oz/ ½ cup red Leicester cheese, grated
1 tbsp poppy seeds
large pinch of paprika
salt and pepper
fresh parsley to garnish

1 Stick the cloves into the onion. Place in a bowl with the carrot, bouquet garni and milk. Heat on HIGH power for 2½–3 minutes. Leave to stand for 20 minutes to allow the flavours to infuse.

2 Trim the base and leaves from the cauliflowers and scoop out the stem using a small sharp knife, leaving the cauliflowers intact. Place the cauliflowers upside down in a large dish. Add the water, cover and cook on HIGH power for 5 minutes until just tender. Leave to stand for 2–3 minutes.

3 Put the butter in a bowl and cook on HIGH power for 30 seconds until melted. Stir in the flour. Cook on HIGH power for 30 seconds.

4 Strain the milk into a jug, discarding the vegetables. Gradually add to the flour and butter, beating well between each addition. Cover and cook on HIGH power for 3 minutes, stirring every 30 seconds after the first minute, until the sauce has thickened.

5 Stir the cheese and poppy seeds into the sauce and season generously. Cover and cook on HIGH power for 30 seconds.

6 Drain the cauliflowers and arrange on a plate or in a shallow dish. Pour over the sauce and sprinkle with a little paprika. Cook on HIGH power for 1 minute to reheat. Serve garnished with fresh parsley.

STEP 2

STEP 2

STEP 3

STEP 4

MOROCCAN VEGETABLES WITH COUSCOUS

An aromatic spicy vegetable stew served on a bed of couscous. For extra heat, try stirring a little chilli sauce into the vegetables before serving.

SERVES 4
PREPARATION: 20 MINS,
  COOKING: 23 MINS

$^1/_2$ aubergine (eggplant), halved lengthwise
  and sliced
350 g/12 oz/1$^1/_2$ cups couscous
5 cardamom pods, split open
1 tbsp chopped fresh thyme
250 g/8 oz baby new potatoes, halved
1 carrot, sliced
1 green (bell) pepper, cut into chunks
1 courgette (zucchini), sliced
1 onion, sliced
60 g/2 oz/$^1/_3$ cup raisins
$^1/_2$ tsp ground cinnamon
1 tsp ground turmeric
1 tsp ground coriander
1 tsp cumin seeds
1 tsp grated ginger root
1 garlic clove, crushed
about 225 g/7 oz/scant 1 cup canned
  chopped tomatoes
300 ml/$^1/_2$ pint/1$^1/_4$ cups hot vegetable stock
salt and pepper
chilli sauce to serve (optional)

1 Place the aubergine (eggplant) in a colander. Sprinkle with salt and leave over a sink for 30 minutes to allow the juices to be drawn out.

2 Cover the couscous with cold water and leave to soak for 10 minutes. Drain and place in a large bowl. Add the cardamom pods and thyme to the couscous. Cover and cook on MEDIUM power for 5 minutes until the grains are soft and swollen. Season to taste.

3 Rinse the aubergine (eggplant) thoroughly to wash off the salt and pat dry with paper towels. Place the aubergine (eggplant) and remaining vegetables in a large bowl.

4 Stir in the raisins, spices, garlic, canned tomatoes and stock. Cover and cook on HIGH power for 18–20 minutes, stirring occasionally, until the vegetables are tender.

5 Season to taste. To serve, make a bed of couscous and spoon on the vegetables. Serve with chilli sauce, if preferred.

STEP 1

STEP 3

STEP 4

STEP 5

SPINACH & NUT PILAU

Fragrant basmati rice with porcini (cep) mushrooms, spinach and pistachio nuts. The pale yellow of the saffron complements the dark green of the spinach, making this a very colourful rice dish.

SERVES 4
PREPARATION: 15 MINS,
    COOKING: 16 MINS

10 g/¹/₃ oz pack dried porcini (cep)
    mushrooms
300 ml/¹/₂ pint/1¹/₄ cups hot water
1 onion, chopped
1 garlic clove, crushed
1 tsp grated ginger root
¹/₂ fresh green chilli, deseeded and chopped
2 tbsp oil
250 g/8 oz generous 1 cup basmati rice
1 large carrot, grated
175 ml/6 fl oz/³/₄ cup vegetable stock
¹/₂ tsp ground cinnamon
4 cloves
¹/₂ tsp saffron strands
250 g/8 oz/6 cups fresh spinach, long stalks
    removed
60 g/2 oz/¹/₂ cup pistachio nuts
1 tbsp chopped fresh coriander (cilantro)
salt and pepper
fresh coriander (cilantro) leaves to garnish

1 Place the porcini (cep) mushrooms in a small bowl. Pour over the hot water and leave to soak for 30 minutes.

2 Place the onion, garlic, ginger, chilli and oil in a large bowl. Cover and cook on HIGH power for 2 minutes.

3 Rinse the rice, then stir it into the bowl with the carrot. Cover and cook on HIGH power for 1 minute.

4 Strain and coarsely chop the mushrooms. Add the mushroom liquid to the stock to make 450 ml/ ³/₄ pint/scant 2 cups. Pour on to the rice. Stir in the mushrooms, cinnamon, cloves, saffron and ¹/₂ teaspoon salt. Cover and cook on HIGH power for 10 minutes, stirring once. Leave to stand, covered, for 10 minutes.

5 Place the spinach in a large bowl. Cover and cook on HIGH power for 3¹/₂ minutes, stirring once. Drain well and chop coarsely.

6 Stir the spinach, nuts and coriander (cilantro) into the rice. Season to taste and garnish with coriander (cilantro) leaves.

> TIP
>
> Use 125 g/4 oz/1 cup button mushrooms, chopped, if dried porcini (cep) mushrooms are unavailable.

CHAPTER FIVE

Desserts

❧

Delicious desserts provide the finishing touch to a meal. From light mousses to the more substantial sponge puddings, these recipes should appeal to most tastes.

Like vegetables, fruit cooks extremely well in the microwave oven. Only a little water needs to be added, allowing the fruit to cook in its own juices. This ensures they keep their shape and texture.

Microwave ovens cannot provide the characteristic browned, crisp texture of crumbles, but this can be overcome by adapting recipes and adding colour and texture through the choice of ingredients. Brown breadcrumbs will add colour while demerara (brown crystal) sugar, crushed biscuits (cookies) and nuts will add texture.

Milk puddings should be cooked on a MEDIUM–LOW power, and in a large container to prevent boiling over. Old-fashioned steamed puddings which usually require hours of cooking are done in a few minutes. Microwave ovens are very useful for drying breadcrumbs, making custard, melting chocolate and gelatine and softening butter.

Opposite: *Fresh and exotic fruit can be used to cook delicious pies and crumbles.*

SPICY PUMPKIN & WALNUT MOUSSE

An unusual mousse made with pumpkin and walnuts and spiced with cinnamon and nutmeg.

STEP 2

STEP 4

STEP 5

STEP 5

SERVES 4
PREPARATION: 15 MINS,
   COOKING: 8 MINS

500 g/1 lb/3 cups peeled pumpkin, diced
5 tbsp water
60 g/2 oz/¹/₃ cup light muscovado (soft
   brown) sugar
60 g/2 oz/¹/₂ cup walnuts, chopped finely
2 tsp ground cinnamon
1 tsp ground nutmeg
1¹/₂ tbsp lemon juice
1 sachet/(envelope) gelatine
3 egg whites
30 g/1 oz/2 tbsp caster (superfine) sugar
60 g/2 oz/2 squares dark chocolate
150 ml/¹/₄ pint/²/₃ cup double (heavy)
   cream, lightly whipped

1 Place the pumpkin in a large bowl with 2 tablespoons of the water. Cover and cook on HIGH power for 6–7 minutes until tender. Leave to stand, covered, for 5 minutes.

2 Tip the cooked pumpkin into a food processor. Add the muscovado (soft brown) sugar, walnuts, spices and lemon juice. Blend until smooth. Alternatively, press the pumpkin through a sieve (strainer). Chop the walnuts very finely then mix into the pumpkin with the muscovado (soft brown) sugar, spices and lemon juice. Transfer to a bowl and leave to cool.

3 Sprinkle the gelatine over the remaining water in a small bowl. Leave to stand for 2 minutes to allow gelatine to 'sponge'. Cook on HIGH power for 30 seconds then stir until dissolved. Stir into the cooled pumpkin and leave until just beginning to set.

4 Beat the egg whites until stiff then beat in the caster (superfine) sugar. Fold into the pumpkin mixture and divide between 4 glasses or serving dishes. Chill until set.

5 Break up the chocolate, place it in a small bowl and cook on HIGH power for 2 minutes. Stir until completely melted. Spread thinly over a baking sheet and leave until set. Using a flat-bladed knife, scrape across the chocolate to make curls.

6 Spoon the cream into a piping (pastry) bag fitted with a large star nozzle (tip). Pipe rosettes on each mousse. Decorate with the chocolate curls.

STEP 1

STEP 2

STEP 3

STEP 6

SPUN SUGAR PEARS

Whole pears poached in a Madeira syrup then served with a delicate spun sugar surround.

SERVES 4
PREPARATION: 18 MINS,
COOKING: 34 MINS

150 ml/¹/₄ pint/²/₃ cup water
150 ml/¹/₄ pint/²/₃ cup sweet Madeira wine
125 g/4 oz/¹/₂ cup caster (superfine) sugar
2 tbsp lime juice
4 ripe pears, peeled, stalks left on
sprigs of fresh mint to decorate

SPUN SUGAR:
125 g/4 oz/¹/₂ cup caster (superfine) sugar
3 tbsp water

1 Mix the water, Madeira, sugar and lime juice in a large bowl. Cover and cook on HIGH power for 3 minutes. Stir well until the sugar dissolves.

2 Peel the pears and cut a slice from the base of each one so they stand upright.

3 Add the pears to the bowl, spooning the wine syrup over them. Cover and cook on HIGH power for about 10 minutes, turning the pears over every few minutes, until they are tender. The cooking time may vary slightly depending on the ripeness of the pears. Leave to cool, covered, in the syrup.

4 Remove the cooled pears from the syrup and set aside on serving plates. Cook the syrup, uncovered, on HIGH power for about 15 minutes until reduced by half and thickened slightly. Leave to stand for 5 minutes. Spoon over the pears.

5 To make the spun sugar, mix together the sugar and water in a bowl. Cook, uncovered, on HIGH power for 1½ minutes. Stir until the sugar has dissolved completely. Continue to cook on HIGH power for about 5–6 minutes more until the sugar has caramelized.

6 Wait for the caramel bubbles to subside and leave to stand for 2 minutes. Dip a teaspoon in the caramel and spin sugar around each pear in a circular motion. Serve immediately, decorated with sprigs of mint.

TIP

Keep checking the caramel during the last few minutes of the cooking time, as it will change colour quite quickly, and it will continue to cook for several minutes after removing from the microwave oven.

STEP 2

STEP 4

STEP 4

STEP 5

MUESLI PUDDING WITH FUDGE SAUCE

A sponge pudding flecked with fruit and nuts and served with a scrumptious fudge sauce.

SERVES 6
PREPARATION: 12 MINS,
COOKING: 10 MINS

FUDGE SAUCE:
30 g/1 oz/2 tbsp butter
175 g/6 oz/1 cup light muscovado (soft brown) sugar
1 tbsp golden (light corn) syrup
6 tbsp single (light) cream
1 tbsp cornflour (cornstarch)
few drops of vanilla flavouring (extract)

PUDDING:
125 g/4 oz/½ cup butter
3 tbsp clear honey
3 tbsp golden (light corn) syrup
60 g/2 oz/⅓ cup dried dates, chopped
60 g/2 oz/⅓ cup sultanas (golden raisins)
60 g/2 oz/⅓ cup glacé (candied) cherries, chopped
60 g/2 oz/½ cup flaked (slivered) almonds
½ tsp ground cinnamon
125 g/4 oz/generous 1 cup rolled oats
125 g/4 oz/1 cup self-raising flour
2 eggs, beaten

1 To make the fudge sauce, mix the butter, sugar, syrup and cream together in a bowl. Blend the cornflour (cornstarch) with a little water and stir into the bowl. Cook on HIGH power for 3–4 minutes, stirring halfway through, until the sugar has dissolved.

2 Add the vanilla flavouring (extract) and leave to stand for several minutes before beating lightly with a balloon whisk to give a smooth consistency.

3 To make the pudding, place the butter, honey and syrup in a large bowl. Cook on HIGH power for 2 minutes until the butter has melted.

4 Stir in the remaining ingredients. Butter a 1.15 litre/2 pint/5 cup pudding bowl, spoon in the pudding and smooth the top. Cook, uncovered, on HIGH power, for 5–6 minutes.

5 Leave the pudding to stand for 5 minutes after cooking. Run a knife around the edge and turn out on to a serving plate.

6 Cut into wedges and serve with the fudge sauce spooned over.

THAI RICE WITH PASSION-FRUIT

Creamy rice pudding made with fragrant Thai rice and spiced with cardamom, cinnamon and bay leaf, served layered with passion-fruit in glasses.

SERVES 4
PREPARATION: 10 MINS,
COOKING: 25 MINS

175 g/6 oz/scant 1 cup Thai or jasmine
  fragrant rice
600 ml/1 pint/2½ cups milk
125 g/4 oz/½ cup caster (superfine) sugar
6 cardamom pods, split open
1 dried bay leaf
1 cinnamon stick
150 ml/¼ pint/⅔ cup double (heavy)
  cream, whipped
4 passion-fruits
soft berry fruits to decorate

1 Place the rice in a large bowl with the milk, sugar, cardamom pods, bay leaf and cinnamon stick. Cover and cook on MEDIUM power for 25–30 minutes, stirring occasionally. The rice should be just tender and have absorbed most of the milk. Add a little extra milk, if necessary.

2 Leave the rice to cool, still covered. Remove the bay leaf, cardamom husks and cinnamon stick.

3 Gently fold the cream into the cooled rice.

STEP 3

4 Halve the passion-fruits and scoop out the centres into a bowl. Layer the rice with the passion-fruit in 4 tall glasses, finishing with passion-fruit. Chill for 30 minutes.

5 Serve decorated with soft berry fruits.

STEP 4

> ### TIP
>
> If you are unable to obtain passion-fruit, you can use a purée of another fruit of your choice, such as kiwi fruit, raspberry or strawberry.

STEP 4

PEAR & BLACKBERRY CRUMBLE

A delicious fruity pudding served with hot custard; a must for any winter's day.

STEP 1

STEP 2

STEP 3

STEP 4

SERVES 4–6
PREPARATION: 15 MINS,
COOKING: 12 MINS

500 g/1 lb ripe pears, peeled and cored
grated rind and juice of 1 small orange
500 g/1 lb/4 cups blackberries
125 g/4 oz/1 cup fresh brown breadcrumbs
60 g/2 oz/¼ cup butter
125 g/4 oz gingernut biscuits (cookies),
   crushed
90 g/3 oz/½ cup demerara (brown crystal)
   sugar

CUSTARD:
2 tbsp custard powder
1 tbsp granulated sugar
600 ml/1 pint/2½ cups cold milk

1 Butter a 1¾ litre/3 pint/2 quart shallow dish. Cut the pears into thick slices. Mix with the orange rind and juice in a large bowl. Cover and cook on HIGH power for 2–3 minutes, until the pears just begin to soften. Add the blackberries, then tip into the buttered dish.

2 Place the breadcrumbs in a bowl and rub in the butter. Stir in the biscuits (cookies) and sugar, breaking up any lumps of breadcrumbs with a fork.

3 Sprinkle the topping evenly over the fruit. Cook on HIGH power for 6–8 minutes. Leave to stand, uncovered, for 10 minutes for the top to become crisp.

4 To make the custard, mix together the custard powder, sugar and a little milk to form a paste. Blend in the remaining milk, whisking well. Cook on HIGH power for 4–6 minutes. Whisk well halfway through the cooking and at the end.

5 Serve the crumble with the hot custard.

TIPS

If gingernut biscuits (cookies) are not available, use graham crackers. If custard powder is not available, use the same amount of cornflour (cornstarch) and add a few drops of vanilla flavouring. You may need to add a little more sugar.

STEP 1

STEP 3

STEP 4

STEP 5

BAKED LEMON & SULTANA (GOLDEN RAISIN) CHEESECAKE

A creamy cheesecake with a sharp citric tang and juicy plump sultanas in an oaty flan case.

SERVES 6
PREPARATION: 25 MINS,
  COOKING: 9 MINS

125 g/4 oz/¹/₂ cup butter
175 g/6 oz/scant 2 cups rolled oats
60 g/2 oz/¹/₃ light muscovado (soft brown)
  sugar
60 g/2 oz/¹/₃ cup sultanas (golden raisins)
3 tbsp lemon juice
175 g/6 oz/³/₄ cup full-fat soft cheese
1 tsp lemon rind
90 g/3 oz/¹/₃ cup caster (superfine) sugar
4 tbsp soured cream
2 eggs, beaten
150 ml/¹/₄ pint/²/₃ cup double (heavy)
  cream, lightly whipped

TO DECORATE:
lemon slices
julienne strips of lemon rind

1 Lightly butter a 20 cm/8 inch flan dish (quiche pan). Melt the butter in a small bowl on HIGH power for 2 minutes. Stir in the oats and muscovado (soft brown) sugar. Press into the flan dish (quiche pan). Chill.

2 Place the sultanas (golden raisins) and lemon juice in a small bowl. Heat on HIGH power for 1 minute. Leave to stand, covered, for 5 minutes so the sultanas (golden raisins) plump up.

3 Beat together the cheese, lemon rind, caster (superfine) sugar, soured cream and eggs until creamy. Stir in the sultanas (golden raisins) and lemon juice.

4 Spoon into the oat case and smooth the top. Cook on MEDIUM power for 6–8 minutes until just set. Leave to cool, then chill.

5 Spoon the double (heavy) cream into a piping (pastry) bag fitted with a large star nozzle (tip). Pipe rosettes around the edge of the cheesecake.

6 Decorate with lemon slices and julienne strips of lemon rind. Cut in wedges to serve.

TIP

If you are watching the calories, use low-fat soft or curd cheese; the cheese cake will be just as good.

INDEX